How to Attract, Lead and Develop People to Deliver Results that Delight You

Leadership Conversations in a Networked Age

Denis Goodchild

Table of Contents

Foreword

Around 100,000 years ago, early human beings began banding together to haul down larger, dangerous mammals and forage collaboratively. This cultural innovation of coordination of action by language has become the foundational innovation and distinctive skill of humankind. As these small bands began to live more permanently in settlements, clans, tribes and nations, so basic coordinated exchanges oriented around fairness evolved into the conventions, norms and institutions that depended upon shared intentions and gave rise to morality and justice.

These fundamental background skills of the human being have underpinned all our radical historical and cultural shifts. They enabled the elaborate rituals for property transfer in Roman times that enabled in turn a break from family and toward city and nation-states. These then ratcheted up into merchant trading and guild societies, modern industrial production lines and today's advanced network economies.

In the 1980s and 1990s, Fernando Flores pioneered the application of new thinking around cybernetics, artificial intelligence and language and invented new ways of coordinating large-scale action and organisations in digitally-enabled, heavily networked work environments. Flores's work with Terry Winograd, professor of computer science at Stanford University, in turn influenced the founders of Google and LinkedIn, which is where Denis picks up the trail.

I first came across Denis in 2012 when we worked together supporting large complex capital projects. Since that first meeting, I have watched as Denis has driven forward his inquiries into the emancipatory power of language and interwoven it with the development of emerging leaders as they come into their own and begin to coordinate large-scale human transformations. In this book, Denis sets out for the first time his inventions that have taken this passion to explore how language underpins today's postmodern, liquid and derivative-based economic life. If leaders are responsible for building the reputational, practical and symbolic capital foundations for their organisation's future financial value, then their linguistic and embodied skills for managing networks of free agents becomes the signature skill of the age. I recommend wholeheartedly Denis's practical account of how leaders can master this new and powerful skill.

Matthew Hancocks, PhD
Missions that Matter Ltd
https://www.afterautonomy.com

Acknowledgements

I would firstly like to recognise and thank the people whose theories and thinking have heavily influenced me and the contents of this book.

The three conversational domains and the thinking on moods are inspired by the work of Fernando Flores. I would also like to recognize Gloria Flores's work on learning and navigating moods. Conversations with Matthew Hancocks helped me see the application of the three conversational domains within the The Networked Age.

Robert Fritz's work on structural tension as a way to clarify and execute goals has been really helpful in both a personal and professional capacity.

Without Peter Thomson's Book Writing Course this book would have remained a "nice to have". I am very appreciative of the support, challenge and patience provided by Peter and his team.

And finally, I would like to thank Chris Goodchild, Cindy Marteney, Judith Ward, Leonie de Bot and Rosalind Frizt for their support and feedback.

Any misinterpretations, mistakes or omissions are all mine.

Testimonials

On behalf of the Astra Zeneca R&D leadership team, I would like to thank you for your dedication and professionalism in making the Constructive Conversations programme such a resounding success. I have personally been delighted at the consistently positive feedback that is reported after every event. The programme is recognised as one of the most successful development interventions we have ever run in AZ and as you know, it is now being adopted in other parts of the business. You have helped our leaders and managers to develop not only the competence but also the courage to tackle sometimes difficult conversations that drive performance and engagement in our workforce. These skills will be of great importance to our managers as we embark on a period of significant change in R&D.

Simon King, R&D HR Vice President, Astra Zeneca, Willmington.

Exceptional client centricity, demonstrates outstanding facilitation skills with multicultural audiences, understands multiple industries and can be sensitive and challenging with colleagues as well as clients.

> Geneva Patterson, Senior Faculty, Center for Creative Leadership, Brussels.

Denis provided a great balance of tough challenge, quiet supportiveness and excellent insight which combined to give an invaluable coaching experience. His expertise in analysing a problem and providing thoughtful approaches to options to resolve it generated results beyond what I imagined would be possible in the time I had with him. His coaching also delivers a range of solid techniques which can be used to continue the good work even after the coaching stops. I believe that the outcomes of the coaching were a key contributor in my promotion from a senior manager role to a Director level position at the end of the time with Denis. I am happy to recommend him highly to anyone.

> Tanya Heath, Director Internal Audit, GVC Holdings, London.

I've worked with Denis close to a year during my transition to a new and challenging role. He helped in my adjustment during a time when I also had a lot of personal changes as well. Thanks to his sincerity, his flexible approach and the mutual trust, we easily shifted to different topics and we talked about what's important or relevant in any given moment in time; whilst not forgetting what we were focusing in developmental terms for the future. He uses a lot of credible evaluation methods, assessment tools and provides reading material to help keep the momentum throughout the relationship. Having a laugh at every meeting is also a very positive bonus. I'd recommend working with Denis when confronting unprecedented business and personal challenges.

Selim Giray, Vice President and General Manager, GlaxoSmithKline, Turkey.

Having gone through many leadership programs, I felt coaching sessions with Denis completely stood apart, since they were flexible & customized. Our sessions focused on the most recent & relevant situations, while keeping in mind the key development goal to be achieved by year end. We worked on many softer aspects of senior leadership like inspiring large teams from a distance, strengthening connect & reflecting authenticity through vulnerability – all of these charted out as clear tangible monthly milestones. If you are looking to enhance soft skills required for effective leadership – Denis can get you to smoothly build on them with simple day-to-day tangible practices that can help you track progress.

Samia Rais, Head of Sales and Marketing Vaccines, GlaxoSmithKline, India.

Denis helped me to lead more from the heart instead of prioritising task based leadership. I now work not only to change minds but win hearts. I am more empathetic and listen in a way that people feel seen and heard, even if I do not always agree with what some say. I am calm and constructive during emotionally charged conversations. Denis helped me see the value of building broader alliances and networks. My team and I have more visible profiles in the business which makes getting things done easier. These changes have helped me implement difficult change faster and more effectively at AstraZeneca, whilst retaining support from my department. I am more rounded as a leader thanks to Denis. A strong recommendation from me.

Dermot McGinnity, Senior Director, Astra Zeneca, Cambridge.

Introduction

The Industrial Age where companies offered life-long employment in exchange for loyal service is over. The stability and certainty that made this possible is being replaced in many industries by a business world which is more VUCA in nature. In other words, more volatile, uncertain, complex and ambiguous.

What is more, people coming on to the job market are not prepared to commit their working lives to one company. The technological developments of the last 30 years have led to a communications revolution. Information on companies, people and jobs is only a few clicks away. We are living through what Reid Hoffman, co-founder of LinkedIn, calls The Networked Age.

What has not changed is organisations need to attract, lead and retain good people.

The further up an organisation you move, the more your performance becomes rated on how you attract, develop and move people through the organisation.

A lot of your work as a leader is about building the competence and confidence of your people. Yes, you will lose people as they outgrow your organisation. This is a good thing. You will attract new people due to your reputation as a leader who develops people spreads through different networks. It is good for your career in the long term!

This book will map out the conversations you need to pay attention to and practise in order to flourish in this Networked Age. It will answer the following questions?

- How do I build and maintain a network that can help me attract people to my organisation?
- How do I gain commitment and achieve clarity on the work that needs to get done?
- How do I support people to achieve results that will delight me and develop them?

My intention in writing this book is to break down and distill these conversations by offering insights, examples and distinctions. The more present you are to the type of conversation you are having the more likely you will get the result you and other people are expecting.

Each conversation belongs to a primary domain. By this I mean the domain where you use it most. And where its use is critical to that domain and the results you want to achieve. It will help you identify the conversation you may not be having or a conversation you need to repeat.

There are three domains where Leadership Conversations for a Networked Age sit.

Conversations to:

- *Connect*, so you have a continuous supply of competent people who are motivated to learn and deliver results for you.
- *Clarify*, so that you have people who are committed and clear on the work that needs to get done.
- *Deliver*, so that you develop your people and get results that will delight you.

Conversations to Connect

*Purpose – To have a continuous supply of
competent people who are motivated to learn
and deliver results for you.*

Be visible and helpful in your networks so that people get to know, like and trust you. Engage with other people's content and share your expertise. This builds good will which makes people more likely to want to help you. What's more, you will increase your chances of getting more qualified applicants for roles in your team.

To achieve anything significant you need other peoples' help. Relationships built on trust and respect form the foundation for effective working relationships. We need to invest time to get to know people so we can decide if and how we can work together. Conversations for Relationship help you do this. This conversation is about creating, deepening and strengthening your working relationships.

How to understand how someone really is matters. In other words, our moods. Our moods determine how we see the future and the actions that make that possible. Our moods impact our results. Most people are unaware of their mood, the impact mood has on them and the people around them. I will introduce the concept of mood and how you can help people understand and change their mood. Mood Checks will uncover how someone really is and help you unlock negative moods.

Learning can be difficult. You want people who learn and develop so that they can do more and bring more value to your team. Moods such as patience, ambition and confidence matter. This conversation will help your people maintain positive moods to accelerate their growth and develop. And ensure people keep learning when they don't feel like it.

People will follow you if they think you understand them. The ability to accurately restate the ideas and feelings of another person to their satisfaction is essential. People will then be more likely to listen and engage with your ideas. With presence, curiosity and practice you will have a skill to improve all your leadership conversations.

You want motivated people working with you, right? People's motivation can change depending on what is happening in their life. It is not your job to fix someone's motivation issue. However, knowing how to talk to someone who has a motivation issue and supporting them is more realistic. People will remember how you treated them during difficult times.

Conversations to Connect are easy to put off. Have at least one conversation in this domain every day. It will pay back handsomely over the coming years. Like the power of compound interest, the effect and benefit increase exponentially. Daily practice and attention to this domain will make you stand out from your peers and as a leader.

Conversations to Clarify

Purpose – To have people who are committed and clear on the work that needs to get done.

This domain builds on the foundation of Conversations to Connect. The pre-project planning phase before you execute and take action.

We will explore how to talk about what is possible. A Conversation for Possibility acts like a bridge taken between an established relationship and to a commitment to do something together. You may or may not decide to recruit someone. You may or may not decide to work with someone on a project.

You decide you want to work with someone. To move from talking to action. There are two actions available to you. To make an offer or a request. This will result in a commitment to action to achieve a goal. The point of making offers and requests is to clarify what outcome will be delivered before taking any action.

If there is mutual interest then a commitment is made to take action and execute to achieve a desired goal in the future. With a shared goal established we move our attention to current reality. A reality check if you like. Where are we now in relation to what we want to achieve? With current reality and the goal clarified, we have a gap between the present and future. A tension that can be resolved through action.

From here, we define the key actions we need to take to move us from current reality to our desired goal.

You may need to off load some of your commitments to your team. You will need to sell this with the benefits to the person clearly defined. When done well everyone benefits. When done badly people feel resentful.

Conversations to Deliver

Purpose –To develop your people and get results that will delight you.

This domain is about execution management. You have clarified your goals, current reality, action steps and who is accountable. Now we move to the conversations that are needed to support and challenge people to deliver on their commitments that were agreed during Conversations to Clarify.

When commitments are not progressing as you would like, you need to let people know. You want to do this in a way that strengthens the relationship and gets people back on track. Tell people when things are going well and being specific on what is going well.

If people are clear on their commitments, Conversations to Deliver become easier. No surprises. A lack of clarity on commitments will cause you problems.

When supporting people, you can either tell them what to think or you can help them think for themselves. One is more directive and the other is more coaching in its approach. Sometimes the most helpful thing you can do is listen and help someone clarify their own thinking. You will move between the two approaches depending on the confidence and competence of the person.

When a commitment is delivered you will need to accept or reject the final result. By accepting we thank the person and let them know what went well and could work better next time. If we reject the final outcome, we need to state what is missing and request further work until we are satisfied.

Conversations to Connect

Purpose – To have a continuous supply of competent people who are motivated to learn and deliver results for you.

Get visible
and be helpful

Since I started consulting back in 2007, I have been very interested in effective marketing principles. At first, for my own business and then for my clients.

I started to notice that senior leaders were getting interested in their personal brand and wanted help on how to get more visibility and influence without being arrogant or obnoxious.

It became clear to me that some marketing principles that have helped me over the years are just as applicable in the context of personal brand building.

The main driver to build a personal brand is for career progression. What is often missed is how a personal brand can also attract a steady flow of good people wanting to work for you. And to fill vacant positions in your organisation quickly with good people.

To do this by avoiding the time, money and risk of a recruiting process for someone outside of your network.

AIDA, a marketing model dating back over 100 years, can help you think about the process of attracting good people to your organisation.

Yes, you will need to invest a few hours a week. It will be worth it!

AIDA stands for Attention, Interest, Desire and Action. It describes the steps people go through when deciding to purchase a product or service.

I have adapted the steps, with people wanting to work with you as the goal. Your target audience are potential recruits and people that can connect you to potential new recruits.

Attention – Attention is about being visible in the places where potential recruits and people that can help you hang out. Where do they hang out? Which forums, networks, alumni groups are they active in? Internally, take on people from graduate and management training programmes for 12-month rotations. These are potential future longer-term recruits. Engage with different people during lunch and coffee breaks. The goal at this stage is for people to know you exist.

Interest – Interest is about doing things where people get to know you. Engage with people's content by 'commenting' and 'liking' posts. Increase your online connections on networking sites, such as LinkedIn, that are relevant to your work. Subscribe to relevant on-line publications and 'comment' and 'like' content. At this stage people know who you are and engage with you in different forums. I recall a manager of mine who was a sponsor of my management training programme. He would attend our networking events and talk to everyone. We got to know him and he got to meet potential future employees for his organisation. The goal at this stage is for people to get to know you.

Desire – Desire is about people having a favourable opinion of you. Be helpful. Create content and discussion threads that are helpful and offer value. Find speaking opportunities and discussion panels where you can offer advice. You are being pro-active and offering value which creates good will. The goal at this stage is for people to know and respect you.

Action – Action is about people wanting to have a discussion with you about a potential role or project. If you do the previous three steps consistently you will have people pro-actively contacting you about work opportunities. You can follow up on these when the time is right. Otherwise make direct and indirect requests to your network about your vacancy. You have built up good will by engaging and helping people. This should lead to some good qualified applications and with a bit of luck the person you are looking for. The goal at this stage is people trusting you enough to recommend people to you AND qualified people contacting you directly about roles in your team.

Yes, this takes time but it pays back in the long term. People get to know you and decide whether they want to work for you before applying for a vacancy. You get the chance to do the same. Both in informal environments. You get qualified candidates. You are more likely to get a good fit this way than looking through applications and interviewing people who you or your network have never met.

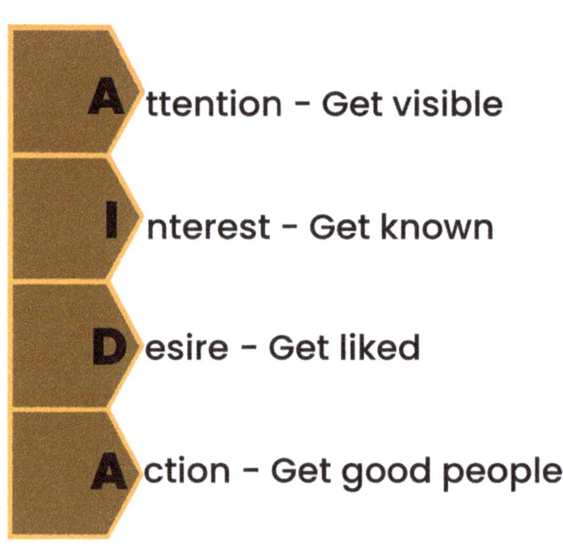

Do we have anything in common? A Conversation for Relationship

Conversations for Relationship answer this question. Do we have enough in common to talk about what may be possible between us?

One client reserves Friday lunch times for this type of conversation. It can be with people who he has never met or to further build his relationship with a colleague. A dedicated time every week which does not get in the way of his already busy schedule.

We do these conversations in our private lives when considering a potential partner over dinner or a coffee.

Relationships are the foundation from which people come together to discuss possible ways of working together.

In this Networked Age these conversations are critical. Some of the conversations will become working relationships. Some not.

You never stop having Conversations for Relationship with people you have shared interests and commitments with. Like peeling an onion, there is always another layer, which in turn unveils another layer.

As a relationship develops, both sides reveal more layers over time and trust builds by fulfilling commitments to each other. This leads to less time wasted and more effective working collaborations.

Conversations for Relationship go beyond surface level conversations about the weather and what you did at the weekend. We want to understand what a person is interested in, cares about and what career experiences they want. We want to know if there is a potential match with what we need.

Don't assume that you know someone because you have been working with them for a few years. People develop and change over time and if you don't ask and spend time in this conversation you may miss important things in people's lives.

Don't mistake this conversation as a nice thing to have! It lays the foundation for effective working relationships.

Relationship building is a task with the goal of relationship building.

"This sounds like a good idea and I am too busy and I don't like networking"

My response is to see it like a task. One you don't like doing which is critical to your success. Just like brushing your teeth gives you good oral hygiene.

When building and developing relationships consider the following questions. Some of the answers may change over time. See the answers you get as a working document.

- What does the person care about?
- What work does the person find meaningful?
- How does the person like to work? Alone, in teams, with who?
- What is the person committed to? Family, caring for a sick parent, managing a junior football team?
- What motivates the person?
- What are their career aspirations?
- What are their current business goals?
- What beliefs does the person hold? About themselves, others and the world?

This information is useful for current and potential future working relationships. Remember, the answers may change over time.

Networking meetings with people you don't know so well are useful. You will discover if you have enough in common to take the conversation further to discuss possible ways of working together. More on this in the next domain.

Some of these conversations may not lead to anything. However, you will always learn something.

Now, some people find relationship building fun and get energised by it. On the other hand, I have senior leader clients who have ignored doing relationship building pro-actively and struggle when they have to start doing it in senior management contexts which are political and multi-cultural.

It's who you know, not what you know...

...So, the saying goes.

People work effectively with people they like, know and trust.

How does this type of conversation fit into your already busy schedule?

Combine them with other activities such as:

- Conferences
- Lunch
- Informal coffee breaks
- Traveling to/from work
- Business trips
- Exercising – playing sport or running
- Taking the first 10 minutes of a 1-1 meeting to ask about non-work interests

Book these meetings in your diary especially if it does not come naturally.

Try "walking the floor" to chat informally with your team. In my first role I recall seeing a senior leader walking around his department and casually chatting with his team who were at their desks. He did this every Monday morning when he was in the office.

This can also work well through direct messaging applications, 1-1 or in a group.

Following and engaging with people on digital platforms and a little research can give a lot of information which can be confirmed during 1-1 conversations.

How do you have a Conversation for Relationship?

- Let the conversation flow and see where it goes without trying to control it.
- Listen out for what the person cares about.
- Ensure a fair share of talking time.
- Share your cares, concerns and desires.
- Listen to understand.
- Be curious.
- Be patient.

Leaders who pro-actively put time aside for Conversations for Relationship reap the rewards of recruiting and retaining good people to their organisation as well as moving their own careers forward.

How are you really doing?

How are you really doing?

Does this conversation sound familiar to you?

"How are you?"

"Fine!"

"How are you?"

"Great thanks!"

The person asking is usually not interested in the answer and the person answering is usually not sharing how they really are.

We need to know how people really are. We have a responsibility for people's well-being and we need to know how things are going with their work.

Working with people's moods is a useful way to support people to think and act in more powerful and effective ways.

So, what do I mean by mood?

We are always carrying a mood around with us. Like carrying a type of weather around. We can feel into our mood. Mood is not our emotions. Emotions are usually directed at someone or something.

For example,

We may be worried because a close family member is in hospital having cancer treatment.

Or we are happy because our favorite sports team has won a tournament.

However, our mood is a combination of how we think and feel about what is possible for us in the future.

For example,

"I am too old to learn a new language".

This person has a mood of resignation. The person is thinking "nothing is going to change. No point of trying as I cannot change anything here". Now, this mood will apply to other aspects of this person's life. This mood impacts what is possible in the future for this person. Learning a new language is not one of them!

If we are NOT conscious of our mood then we can experience life as happening to us and being powerless to affect any change.

We cannot control the mood we fall into. However, we can navigate our way into more productive moods.

By understanding and talking about mood we can help our people take more effective action in their work. We can help people become aware of what is stopping them take action.

Moods can be split into negative and positive. Negative moods restrict what is possible for us to achieve. Positive moods support us in creating and achieving things that matter to us. Each mood has a story attached to it. In other words, what we think about when we are in a particular mood.

The chapters, processes and distinctions on mood have been taken and adapted from Fernando Flores in his book Conversations for Action and Collected essays. A book I would highly recommend.

Some typical moods in the business world:

Positive Moods	Negative Moods
Ambition – I see opportunities and I am ready and prepared to take action.	*Arrogance* – There is nothing new here for me. What you say may be interesting, I already know what is going on. You are wasting my time.
Acceptance – The future is uncertain and unpredictable. Good and bad things will happen and I am grateful for life.	*Confusion* – I don't understand what is going on here or what to do about it and I don't like it. Get me out of here.
Curiosity - I am not sure what is going on here and there is something to learn here which I like.	*Anxiety* – I don't know what I am doing and I may make mistakes, which is a bad thing. It is better to not try than make mistakes.
Confidence – I have successful past experience and competence in this area. There may be some learning involved and I know that if I ask for help, I will get it.	*Frustration* – Things are not going as quickly as they should do. This is not working as it should.
Patience – Achieving anything significant takes time and I accept this. Things take the time they take.	*Resignation* – Nothing is going to change here. There is no point in trying to do anything as I cannot change anything.
Trust – I believe you are sincere and can deliver on what you promise.	*Distrust* – I don't think you intend to do what you said you would do. Or I don't think you are competent enough to do what I need from you.
Resolution – Something is possible for me here. I am going to take action to make it happen.	

It can be helpful sharing these moods and associated stories so that people have a language for them. I usually ask for people's moods at the beginning of a conversation and the story behind the moods. No further discussion.

For example:

"I am feeling overwhelmed at the moment. I have changed job and I still have some responsibilities for my previous role. It is too much at the moment."

Below are two examples of how to affect a person's mood.

You ask someone to present at your manager's team meeting. It is her first time presenting at this meeting. She says she is worried and questions whether she is ready to do this. In talking with her it becomes clear she is in a mood of anxiety about doing this. You believe she can do it. While it is natural for her to be nervous, you are there to support her and the fact that she has done this in previous roles provides a good reason for her to go into this with a mood of confidence. You want to challenge someone's mood if there is a good reason to do so. In other words, you can make a case for why another mood is more appropriate and more helpful, too.

You have appointed an ambitious new country manager. The country team she has inherited is conservative and does not like a lot of change. After two months she is sharing her frustration with you that the changes she wants to make are not happening fast enough. A classic mood of frustration. You notice she has made progress and are satisfied, as this is her first general manager's role. Pointing this out and opening the possibility that a mood of patience and resolution would be more helpful due to the context she is operating in.

We are not trying to change anyone's belief when working with moods. It is more about making people aware of their mood. This can be enough sometimes. Then, challenging them to see other possible moods that are more realistic and/or helpful in the context they are operating in.

When you notice a negative mood with someone that seems to hang around, the following steps can help. Help someone observe their mood and the opinions that support them. This way you can begin to challenge and shift their opinions and therefore their mood.

Discussing a negative mood

1. Awareness
Become aware of your body sensations and feelings. What do you notice?

2. Choice
Are you ready to make a commitment to alter this mood? If yes, continue to number three; otherwise, by when will you decide? Or, are you at peace with this situation and do not see a need to alter your mood?

3. Investigation – What or who is the mood about?
What is the story you tell yourself while in this mood? Is it your opinion or a fact?

If it is your opinion, can you offer some evidence to back it up?
What standards are you using?

Are they shared by the people you work with?

If it is a fact? Is it true or false?
If true, what is it going to take for you to accept this?
If you realise the fact is false, does this shift your mood? If not, is your negative mood really about something else?

4. Plan for action
What is missing?
Do you need to ask for help, make an offer, pull out of a commitment or make a new commitment?
Do you need to make a complaint?
Do you need to apologise?

5. Take action
With whom and by when?

6. Complete
Have new opportunities opened up as a result for completing this exercise?

If so, what request or offer could you make now?

I don't like being incompetent

In this Networked Age ambitious and motivated people look for leaders who will support them in their growth and development. These people will be with you for a maximum 2-3 years before taking on their next assignment. If you can create a culture of growth and development you will attract good people.

One of the best ways to develop people is to give them work that challenges and stretches them. This will usually mean a drop in performance as new capabilities are developed to meet the demands of the work. And usually, negative moods such as confusion, anxiety and frustration are experienced.

If you want to become good at anything or take a bigger job with more responsibility and complexity, performance usually goes down, to then go up further than the previous highest point.

This is best exemplified in sport when golfers change their swing, footballers try a new position, tennis players change their service action or introduce a new shot into their repertoire.

Anyone that has become good at anything was not very good at it at some time.

To become good, we will experience periods of incompetence and not knowing.

During this period of development, we want to encourage people to become excellent beginners and cultivate moods of curiosity, ambition and patience.

We need to understand and help our people to learn how to learn and support them through the emotional rollercoaster of learning.

Now, you need to be more competent yourself or engage someone in your team who is in order to be able to assess development and performance and offer the right support.

Have an open and honest conversation around current competence levels, what the next level of competence is, how long it usually takes and what support you will be giving the person to develop.

We need positive moods and supporting opinions that are rooted in realistic standards.

I do NOT mean thinking positive or taking on positive beliefs.

Our job is to point out unproductive moods and opinions along with the unrealistic standards that support them.

A few examples:

1 - Unproductive mood – Frustration
Opinion – I tried to do this. I am never going to be able to do this. I expected to be able to do this already. I am not getting this as fast I should. This is not working as it should.

Standard – Being competent is bad. Making mistakes is bad.

Response - We expect to be able to pick up things quickly and become impatient and frustrated if we don't. The expectation is unrealistic and unfair a lot of the time.

2 - Unproductive mood – Resignation
Opinion – This is not going to work. I am not going to be able to get good at this. There is not much point in trying.

Standard – I should already be competent and if not, I should step aside.

Response - Learning a new skill or being competent in a more senior role takes time. We need support and help which we are expected to ask for.

3 - Unproductive mood – Lack of confidence (Insecurity).
Opinion – I need to get good as this quickly by myself and avoid showing weakness.

Standard – People expect me to be good at this and I should already be competent.

Response - The expectation of others is usually incorrect. People generally enjoy helping others when asked. People can get frustrated if you don't ask for help and shut them out.

You want to help someone with a negative mood to become aware of it, understand the unrealistic nature of the standard and choose a better mood for learning.

Cultivating moods of patience, resolution and ambition can be helpful in all three examples.

Questions to ask when someone is experiencing negative moods:

What mood are you in?

What is the story attached to the mood (the opinion)?

What standards are you holding yourself to?

Is the standard fair and realistic?

Would you have the same standards for other people?

What mood would be more helpful?

You want to help someone with an unhelpful mood become aware of it, understand the unrealistic nature of the standard and choose a better mood for learning.

This is exactly what I mean

Getting good at leadership conversations means getting good at not talking. Understanding and showing you understand another person is critical.

This skill applies to ALL your leadership conversations.

Steven Covey dedicates one of his habits to understanding the person you are talking to. "Seek first to understand and then be understood" is one of Steven Covey's Seven Habits of Highly Effective People. A classic management book I would highly recommend.

Arguably the most important skill in having conversations that matter is our ability to hear what the person is trying to say. Showing them that we understand so they can relax and talk knowing that we get them. Like an endangered species it can be hard to find people who give their undivided attention to someone when they are talking.

You will stand out if you can offer this in your leadership conversations.

To do this really well, practise being more present and cultivate a mood of curiosity.

Let us start with how you can be more present.

Presence

Being fully present with people is difficult. We are bombarded by distractions. However, we can do something about it.

There are two types of distractions. External and internal. We want to reduce the impact of both.

External distractions are people and technology.

You can reduce the external distractions by taking practical steps such as having your phone on silent mode, closing the door, putting down your laptop screen, asking not to be disturbed.

During sessions with teams and groups this is the time laptop screens go down and mobile phones get placed in bags. ☺

Internal distractions refer to how our attention wanders away on to another subject. It could be another meeting we are worried about, what we are going to have for dinner or something we remembered we need to do before we leave work.

You can't stop your attention wandering. The key thing is to be able to bring back your attention as soon as you notice it going somewhere else.

People know when you are present and listening and when you are not.

"It is amazing how much MORE people talk and share when you give them your undivided attention". A common response to practising presence.

Who would not want more information from people in their teams and network?

So how can you be more present?

A useful practice is to take a mindful minute before each meeting.

When you have back-to-back meetings, your mind is like tea leaves in a cup after having hot water poured on it. Tea leaves flying around represent your thoughts. The mindful minute, and I mean 1 minute, helps let some of the tea leaves fall to the bottom of the cup and settle so you have less thoughts flying around your mind. This will make you more present to the next person you are speaking with.

A practice such as the mindful minute will help calm your nervous system down. It will settle your thoughts so you have less going round in your head.

The Mindful Minute

You can do this almost anywhere without bringing attention to yourself. You don't have to be seated crossed legged on your desk with your thumbs and little fingers touching each other and eyes closed to do this.

I recommend you are seated when you do it.

- Sit up with a straight back. Imagine someone is pulling you up from the top of your head. Get firm contact on the floor with your feet.
- Take one breath. Then inhale…and then exhale. Make the breath a little longer than you usually do.
- Take out your phone and set the timer for one minute.
- Start the timer and start breathing. Count how many breaths you take in one minute. One breath includes an inhale and an exhale.
- If you have any tension or tightness breathe into it.

- Focus on your breathing. Breathe in and breathe out. You can say to yourself "breathe in……breathe out" while you are doing it.
- So, let's say you took 11 breaths. This is the number of breaths you will take when you practise your mindful minute.

If you find the mindful minute helpful you may want to consider a meditation or yin yoga practice as a way to calm your nervous system down.

Curiosity

Curiosity is about not knowing and being ok with it.

Be genuinely interested in what the person is telling you. Even if it does not interest you!

You do this without judging the person. Judging someone continuously is the surest way to get someone to shut up and not share their thoughts and feelings.

Don't try and fake this because you will get caught out eventually.

You are being curious for the sake of being curious. See where it takes you.

Start with a blank piece of paper.

Someone starts talking and you start filling the page with what they are saying.

Picture it and get curious about what you are seeing. What is missing in the picture?

Ask a question about what is missing.

When you are being curious you don't have to fix anything. If someone asks for your advice, you can share your thoughts.

You want to help someone make sense of their own thoughts and thinking. Your presence and curiosity can make the difference between someone getting a clearer understanding of an issue or not.

This is all that people need sometimes. Someone to run their idea by and check it makes sense to another human being.

"I don't feel like I am doing anything". You are doing a lot.

It can be helpful to have some focus areas when listening, which can be explored if relevant.

The following are some areas to focus your curiosity:

Values – What matters most to this person? What do they value most? Driving a business unit forward, being a part of team, getting home at 17:00 to eat dinner with the kids? If someone is behaving in a way that contradicts their values this would be worth exploring.

Commitments – What commitments does he have? Work, partner, kids, sick parent, charity work? People are often over-committed. They have too much on. Taking back control and consciously deciding on what to commit to can help.

Beliefs - Explanations for how things are. "The executive team are only interested in themselves", "I can never have that position", "I don't have time for this". Beliefs are true to the person holding them. Usually taken from other people and without much thought. Pointing out and critically looking at our beliefs and challenging the utility of them can open up new ways of thinking and acting in the world.

Feelings – Feelings are a door into what is really going on for someone. Knowing the feeling alone is not very helpful. So, if someone is frustrated, we want to find out what is causing the frustration.

"So, you sound frustrated".

"Yeah, you can say that again".

"Why are you frustrated?"

"Well, at the last toll-gate meeting..."

Concerns – What is on someone's mind. Hitting the numbers at year end; how to manage a poor performing colleague; demotivated teenager who does not want to study; a marriage which has lost its spark and fun. Now, you don't have to be able to solve every concern a direct report has. Taking an interest and caring about a colleague's concerns is important. Showing that you care is not only about performance. It is about them as a person and the things they care about.

Energy - Does someone's energy match what they are saying? Body movements, speed of talking. Repeat back HOW someone is coming across can help someone reflect on how they feel and think about something. Don't assume that you know what is going on. Check it out!

For example:

"You sound really excited."

"You seem impatient around this task."

Now, to develop more presence and curiosity takes practice and attention.

You have two ears and one mouth. Use them in that proportion.

Summarising the key elements of what someone has said is a very powerful way of showing your understanding. People relax and open up more when they think we have understood. This gives you more information and data to better understand the situation. This will result in better decision making around issues.

For example:

Anna – I am really stressed right now with this ERP implementation. I am working full time and want to spend more time with the family. The kids are young and need a lot of attention and we have just started renovating the kitchen.

Peter – You have a lot on right now and not enough time with your kids.

Anna – That is right. You know, what' s more...

And the conversation continues.

It is not my job to motivate you

We will experience highs and lows in our life and at work. Nothing new here.

People will approach you to talk about potential next moves in their career before, during and after working with you.

And, you have a responsibility to be aware and support your people during difficult times.

You cannot motivate someone to do something. You can create the conditions for people to do work that motivates them. Motivation is intrinsic and involves doing something because it is personally rewarding. You can inspire someone.

Let's take a look at the research on motivation and then detail some questions you can use to find out what drives someone.

In 1959 Frederick Herzberg's classic study published in the Harvard Business Review found that factors that led to job satisfaction - motivators - and those that led to job dissatisfaction - hygiene factors - were different.

His study found that motivators, which can lead to increased motivation are intrinsic such as achievement, recognition for achievement, responsibility, growth and development.

Hygiene factors are extrinsic and will lead to job dissatisfaction such as company policy, administration, supervision, team environment, working conditions, status, salary and security. Job dissatisfaction means if we don't take care of these factors, we risk people feeling job dissatisfaction. We won't increase motivation; however, we will avoid dissatisfaction. Let me give you an example.

Motivators

Achievement, recognition for achievement, responsibility, growth and development.

Hygiene Factors

Company policy, administration, supervision, team environment, working conditions, status, salary and security.

When it comes to money, offering a competitive compensation package is important. We want to take the discussion of money off the table to avoid it causing job dissatisfaction. Money, is rarely a motivator in the long term. The exception is in mechanical, rule-based manual tasks which are straightforward to do.

In 2009, Dan Pink in his book Drive argued a similar case to Hertzberg about the intrinsic nature of motivation. He cites studies in the fields of Economics and Psychology, concluding that what actually motivates us are intrinsic factors of Mastery, Autonomy and Purpose. Open-source software such as Linux and companies setting aside time for people to do side projects to innovate new services are modern day examples. His RSA animated talk offers a short summary of his research. Search "RSA Dan Pink" to find it.

Hertzberg characterized motivation as someone having their own generator powered by themselves without outside stimulation. Action, in other words, being self-generated.

We all have a generator. The question to explore is,

What are the aspirations and values that power the generator?

If you have someone who starts to underperform or behaving strangely and it is not a competence issue, she may be experiencing a motivation issue, something which is personal to her.

This is where listening and getting curious is important as it is something personal to the person. We don't want to assume and take action which may not actually help the situation.

Having Motivators and Hygiene factors in the back of your mind can be helpful.

What else is the person committed to outside of work? Family, friends, interests connected to clubs or associations. Has anything changed?

It's not your job to solve non-work issues. Taking an interest and care of their overall well-being is.

Sometimes people just want someone to share an issue with. For example, someone is going through a divorce. It may be an issue with another colleague or project which is affecting someone's mood.

Or someone may have lost the purpose of a piece of work and how it connects to your strategy. Reminding someone on why a project is important to you and the organisation can be helpful. This will help someone understand and reconnect with a piece of work and find their motivation to engage with it.

Key messages from Conversations to Connect

- Get visible and be helpful in networking forums. This will make attracting and recruiting qualified and good people a lot easier.
- Understanding the cares and concerns of people is essential. We do this through Conversations for Relationship to help us decide if we will commit to working together.
- Finding out what mood someone has tells us how somebody really is and what action is possible for them. We can help people understand and change their mood.
- People learn best in moods of curiosity, patience and ambition. Being incompetent and making mistakes is part of learning and normal.
- Presence and a mood of curiosity is critical to understanding someone. People are more likely to listen to you when they feel you understand their situation.
- You cannot motivate someone. People feel unmotivated sometimes. People have to find their own motivation.
- Help people connect with their aspirations and values.

Join Leadership Tuesdays to receive my weekly insights on leadership, navigating change and high-performing teams. Go to leadership4managers.com and sign up.

Conversations to Clarify

What is possible here? – A Conversation for Possibility

So, you have an idea or a project that you want to involve someone in. A Conversation for Possibility comes about through established working relationships or newer relationships that show potential to become working relationships. Before committing to doing anything together with someone, this stage is about exploring what may be possible.

This is similar to brainstorming or networking. Is there a good fit for what you want to achieve?

Conversations to Connect, when practiced, will make choosing who to talk to a lot easier.

If you have people in your organisation then start there. If the person does not exist in your network, then you can make a request to your external network about the type of person you want to talk to.

A few examples;

- Now, you will have experienced this yourself when talking to someone about a shared sporting interest and you realise that you support the same team. The discussion leads to another conversation about the possibility of watching a match together.

- You have a talented and ambitious person from your company's management development programme who has been working in your function for the last 6 months. You want to talk to her to find out more about her future goals and talk about a potential permanent role.

- You have a new project that needs managing. You have someone in mind who you know and trust. You want a conversation to talk about the project outcomes and their views on it. You are checking out if they are right for the role.

- You want to discuss a new product or service idea. You bring together a group of people who have a shared interest to discuss ideas around what is possible. You want this to be as broad as possible, holding nothing back. Getting as many opinions out there as possible.

This conversation can be standalone. You can make it clear to people that this is case. This will give you time to reflect and consult others on your thoughts before committing to anything.

It is important to keep a certain amount of focus and boundaries around what you are talking about so the conversation does not go too far off track. You also want an open and exploratory discussion. If an opportunity or possibility arises then you can arrange to talk about how to move forward. If not, then no further action is needed. Be clear whatever you decide. People appreciate being kept updated.

You can commit to commit. In other words, agree to get back to someone on a decision.

I will let you know this Friday whether you will be called for an interview. This is to avoid having to say YES or NO immediately when you need some time to think.

Now, you may end up deciding not to move forward with anything from the conversation. That is a decision. Or you may end up committing to take action. We will talk about this in the following chapters.

I would be delighted if you can do this for me

So, through a Conversation for Possibility you decide you want to commit to work together. Even if the goal is clear for you and you know what you need, the person you are talking with may not have that clarity.

This conversation is about agreeing to commit to action which will result in an outcome that will satisfy you. If you are being asked to commit to something then this conversation is just as relevant. You want to satisfy your boss, right?

From a Conversation for Possibility there are two ways you can move to action.

Make a request or make an offer.

Let's start with requesting. This conversation is about requesting and clarifying what will delight you.

If you are going to achieve anything significant or meaningful in life you are going to need help to do it. Jesus, Mohammed, Mother Theresa, Marie Curie, Mandela and Gandhi to name but a few engaged the help of other people to achieve things.

When you are setting expectations and goals, the elements of requesting can be helpful. Even small requests such as asking someone to fix the end of year activity are included here.

Requesting is as important when agreeing on goals and targets. This includes cascaded goals. Even though you are the boss, you still want people to be positive and motivated to achieve the goals for the year.

Some people find requesting things easier than others. This could be down to a culture of individualism or heroic leadership in the western world; where the individual leader is seen as the person who achieves – or at least is expected to achieve - everything alone through hard work and will power. Or that asking other people is perceived as a weakness or a sign of incompetence.

Conversations to Connect and Clarify

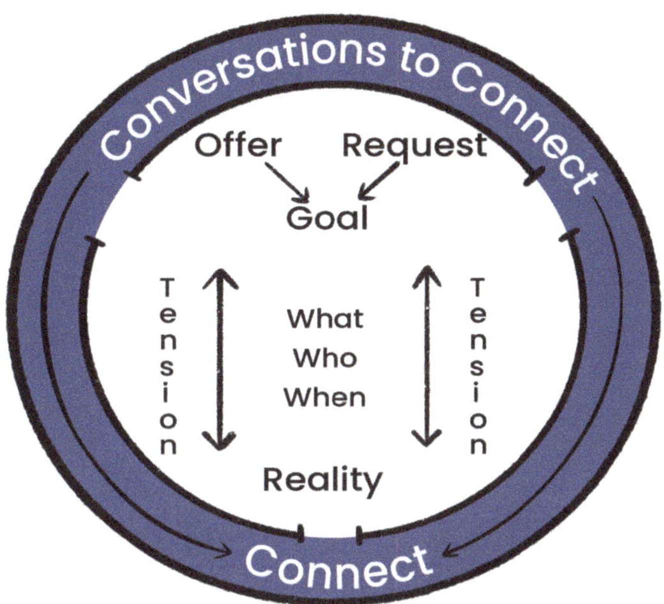

Requesting is a skill. You are requesting someone to commit to do something with an expected goal in mind.

The following is a list of questions to help you structure and focus your request:

What are you concerned about?

You want to get to what is on your mind.

For example, we are going to miss our budget for product x this month.

Or, we need to better engage the local community.

Now, you making a request based on a concern is OK. This gets people thinking about how they could help you without dictating exactly what needs doing. This is likely to lead to more options being presented back to you, some of which you may not have considered yourself.

What is missing?

When making a request you are usually asking for something that does not exist.

Can you decrease our indirect purchasing costs by 2.5% this year?

Can you book a meeting with Erika for an update on project Hercules?

Can you find one new revenue stream in your service offerings for the new financial year?

Why is this important to you?

For anyone to take your request seriously they need to know why it is important. Should they take you seriously?

What will you do with the information and output they provide you? Asking for a report, which then gets ignored or not used annoys people and will ultimately lead to your requests being ignored in return.

Who would be a good fit for this request?

Who is competent to help you with this? Is the person you are asking capable of doing what you ask of them? It can also be something that will challenge and stretch someone. People will be wondering "why me "? Let them know.

How can you communicate your request in a language that is understood?

Will the person understand the language you are using? By this, I mean technical language and abbreviations. R&D, Marketing, HR, Engineering and Legal have ways of communicating which might as well be a foreign language! Are you requesting something from someone from a similar background or not? Adapt and simplify your language as needed.

What outcome will make you satisfied? Be specific.

You are asking for somebody's commitment here. Be as clear as you can on what will make you satisfied. You could even give two levels of satisfaction. Satisfied and delighted. If someone is going to invest their time in helping you, which most people will happily do, they will want to satisfy your request. Let them know what will make you satisfied.

What communication medium is most appropriate?

Face to face, email, direct messaging, traditional mail.

Which is the best way to communicate your request?

Goal-setting would ideally be face-to-face, for example. Even for simple requests such as meetings, be sure to get confirmation that your message has been received. You sending a message with a request does not equal your request being received or accepted. "I sent you an email" does not count!

You are more likely to under-communicate than over-communicate.

Getting clear about what is being asked for, by when and to what quality is important here. If you agree to do something, you will be making a commitment to deliver on the request.

Now there are four things that can happen when we make a request. We get:

1- Commitment – "Yes OK, I will organize the end-of -year party!"
2- A No – "I organized the team dinner last year and I would prefer not to do it this year"
3- A counteroffer – "I organised it last year, I can take it next year."
4- Commit to commit (I will get back to you) – "We may be away for the dinner this year. Can I check my diary at home and get back to you on Friday lunch time?

It is important to be open and honest during this phase. Can the person commit to what is being asked with all the other commitments they have? What room for negotiation do you have? Can you de-prioritise other commitments for the same person? Saying "No" should be an option. Be concerned and curious if "No" becomes the standard answer to reasonable requests.

You will need to get clear on your goal and what you want, timelines and quality expected so that when you get commitment, you and the person actioning your request know what success looks like.

Responses to Offers and Requests

Commitment – "Yes, OK I will do it"

No – "I cannot do it"

Counter offer – "No and how about…"

Commit to commit– "Cannot answer now. I will get back to on…"

Would you be interested in…?

The other way of committing to action is to make an offer.

We are being made offers all the time.

Pizza delivery in 30 minutes or your money back.

Express delivery within 24 hours of your order.

Two for the price of one until Sunday.

With offers you are committing to make something happen and you need a person with authority, usually your manager, to accept it.

With a request you want someone to commit to do something that will satisfy you.

When making an offer you are committing to do something to satisfy someone else.

All the elements of requesting are relevant for making an offer.

Let's take an example of a leadership team member offering to deliver a code of ethics policy to be launched on the 12th January.

What concern or issue is your offer solving?

I can write a Code of Ethics that everyone in the organisation signs up to in order to protect our reputation and avoid any more bad publicity.

What resources do you need?

I need feedback from all key functions before presenting back.

What will you deliver? (Quality, time and benefits)

A first draft of the code of ethics — with feedback integrated - to discuss at the leadership meeting on the 5th November in preparation for a launch on 12 January.

Why is it important?

The recent scandals, which were well publicised globally, have damaged our reputation as an ethical market leader in our industry.

What outcome will satisfy the person you are accountable to?

The CEO asked that all key function heads are consulted before presenting back a first draft.

How will you communicate the offer?

In this case it was during a face-to-face meeting. Simple offers such as organising the logistics for an off-site team meeting can be made by email and followed up with different communication media.

Now there are four things that can happen when we make an offer. We get:

1- Commitment – "Yes OK, take the lead this with this and launch it on the 12 January.
2- A No – "Let's hold off with this for now"
3- A counter offer – "Yes we need to take action and it is very urgent. Can you deliver this by 12 December"?

4- Commit to commit (I will get back to you) – "Lets discuss this again at the next leadership team meeting and decide then on what to do?

By making a request or an offer we have established the goal we want to achieve. From here we want to understand where we are now in relation to our goal in order to help us plan what to do.

That is great and we need a reality check

You have a commitment to a goal. You got this by making a request or an offer.

Now we want to understand our starting point. In other words, the current reality.

Your understanding of current reality will influence the offers and requests you make.

Doing a current reality check before making an offer or accepting a request is recommended. Otherwise, you many need to renegotiate what you have agreed on or fail to achieve what you want in terms of time, quality and cost.

This can be a standalone conversation. You could also start with a current reality check conversation and then have a Conversation for Possibility. This may or may not lead to a request or an offer.

A reality check is about getting clear on current reality. When we are clear on current reality there will be a gap between where we are now and our goal. This will create tension, energy and a need to plan how to move forward. Think of it like you are holding arrow in a bow, pulled back, ready to release and pointed at its destination.

There is a practical part of detailing current reality and different ways we can see current reality.

Let's start with a practical part.

Now, there is a lot of focus in the business world around taking action towards pre-defined goals and achieving objectives.

However, there seems to be less focus on defining the starting point. Where are we in relation to what we want to achieve?

This is important and critical. A clear and honest assessment of current reality combined with what you want to achieve helps us define what we need to do to get what we want.

So why is getting clear on current reality useful?

By doing this we create what Robert Fritz calls structural tension between where we are now and where we want to be. Structural tension seeks equilibrium. Structural tension exists all around us.

In physics, structural tension explains how a plane lifts off the ground. The air flows faster on top of the wing which leads to lower pressure than the air flowing under the wing. This difference in pressure creates a force on the wing which lifts the plane off the ground.

When we are hungry there is tension between the amount of food we want and the amount of food we have in the body. This tension seeks equilibrium because of the difference. So, we eat something and that resolves the tension.

Films use this type of tension to keep us engaged. The tension between the good guys and the evil guys. Who will come out on top? Two guys competing over the girl. Who gets the girl? What is going to happen? We want to know. Our minds seek equilibrium between the amount of information we have and the amount of information we want. In other words, we want the tension to be resolved.

Let's take the code of ethics example and say on this occasion that the CEO has asked you – made a request – to lead a project to launch a company-wide code of ethics.

Goal – Launch a code of ethics document by 12 January.

Current Reality – 4 months till go-live; strong sponsorship from leadership team to launch this; no team in place; high profile project; successful result will be good for my reputation; tension between Commercial and Compliance heads around what to include in the document; project execution during Q4 and we are behind budget.

Now, there is a tension between current reality and the goal. A tension by its very nature seeks equilibrium in the form of its resolution: the achievement of your goal.

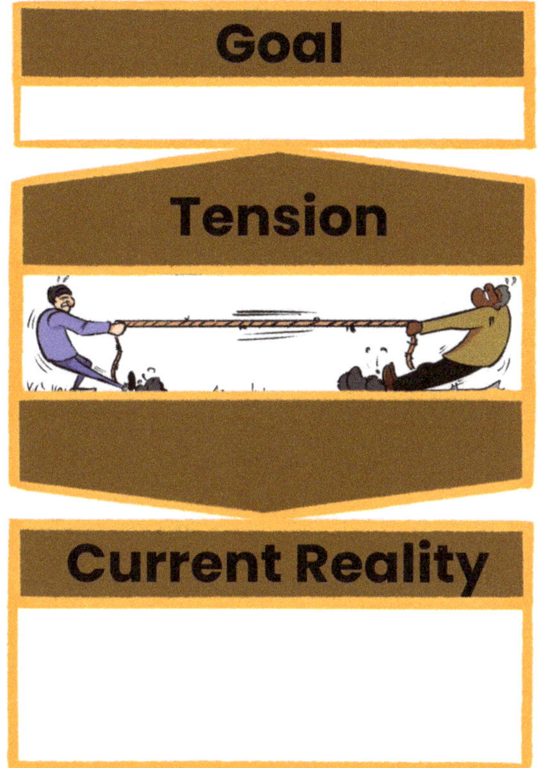

I rarely see much attention paid to current reality in my consulting work. All too often, a direction is set and action is taken. This reduces the chances of achieving goals. Current reality catches up with us eventually.

You want to include as much as possible in reality to help plan the actions needed to achieve your goal. This will help create the necessary tension to start planning how to move towards your goal.

The other part of getting to current reality is helping people see their reality in a way which is not too detailed or unfocused.

Robert Fritz in "The Path of Least Resistance for Managers" uses a video camera analogy to describe three common ways in which people view current reality; The Closeup, Medium Shot and Long Shot. He argues that The Medium Shot is the most useful with its attention on shapes, trends and patterns.

The Closeup – Immediate Events and Obsessive Detail.

Some people can be very detailed focused. With a very limited and short-time horizon focusing on immediate events and the day-to-day. They are zooming in and struggle to see the context of what they are talking about and pull conversations back to shorter time horizons which feels comfortable for them. Obsessing over details without understanding the context in which they sit.

The Vice President for the Nordics region needs to reduce the headcount in his region. The head of Finland is complaining that he cannot reduce the people in his team and defends his position without seeing the bigger picture of headcount reduction in the whole region.

You are talking about your 3–5-year strategy with the team. A team member takes a current issue he is facing, for example, with a government authority, and focuses everybody's attention on it. He is missing out the impact of other external stakeholders and the change in business strategy.

Our job here is help people take a step back to see the bigger picture. To see the forest AND the trees. Helping them put their details in the wider context of the business.

The Long Shot – chronic vagueness.

On the other extreme, you have people who describe their reality in abstract, lofty language. Continuous improvement, agile, growth mindset, social media or digital strategy are examples of concepts that, if not specified, make it hard to do anything with. A way of describing how the world is without being grounded in how things currently are. It can sound very inspiring at first and frustrating over time as the language remains vague and unspecified and nothing of importance actually gets done.

We want people to get more concrete and grounded and move away from abstract concepts that are not connected to reality. Without a clear view of current reality, achieving goals is difficult.

The following questions can help someone see reality more clearly.

What do you mean by creating a more agile organization?

How are things going right now? What is working, not working?

Where are we now in relation to our goal of reducing costs by 4% this year?

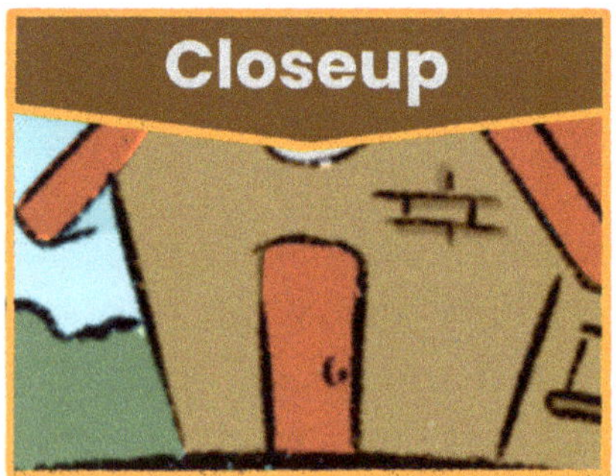

The Medium Shot – shapes, patterns and trends.

This view is about seeing the forest AND the trees. It is about seeing detail in context without getting lost in it, while holding a clear picture of what you want to achieve in relation to where you currently are. Seeing the result of actions and noticing patterns of what is working and what is not working.

Some useful questions to support people see current reality through a medium shot:

- What patterns are you noticing?
- Where do you need to put your attention in the coming months?
- What implications do the trends you are noticing have on what you want to achieve?

The answers to these questions can be included in where you record current reality.

Seeing how we are doing locally fits into the national and global strategy. Zooming in and out as needed to keep a clear view of current reality and taking action accordingly.

Having a clear goal from either a request or offer and a clear view of current reality is not something you do once and move on. It is something you come back to and update as you move towards your goal. Current reality never sits still!

Now we have our goal and current reality set out we move to the actions needed in order to bridge the gap between the two.

What, who and by when

When you have your goal and current reality clearly defined you have created structural tension. The tension of being somewhere (current reality) and wanting to be somewhere else (goal).

With these two elements in place, you can start to plan the steps needed to move you from your current reality to your goal.

So, you have a clear idea of the goal.

You have a clear idea of where you are – current reality – in relation to the goal you want.

There is a discrepancy between your current reality and the goal. What actions need to be taken to bridge the gap between your current reality and the goal?

A master structural tension chart can help. A master structural tension chart to define the high-level actions and who is accountable for achieving them.

Let's take our example of creating the code of ethics (see illustration). With this high-level plan, we need to make a request from the people we have allocated actions for. For example, FT regarding the communication plan. We are looking for a commitment from FT to deliver and manage a communication plan.

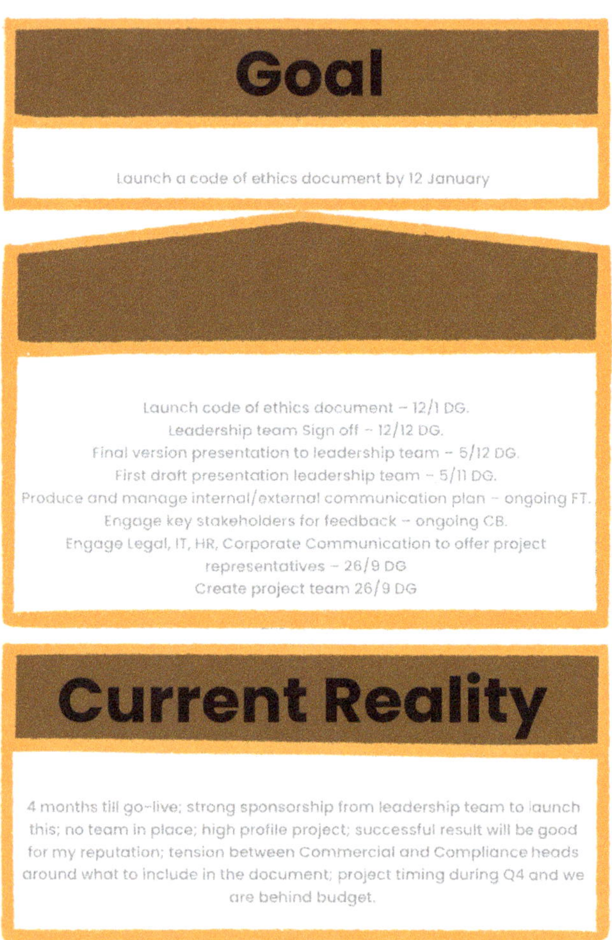

You could also request a structural tension chart from FT, which you can use as a way of tracking progress and aligning FT's work with the project.

Each one of the action points if needed can lead to another structural tension chart with a goal, current reality and action steps. This is called telescoping. This can help you see the connections between different work streams and any changes that are needed to avoid duplication and increase effectiveness.

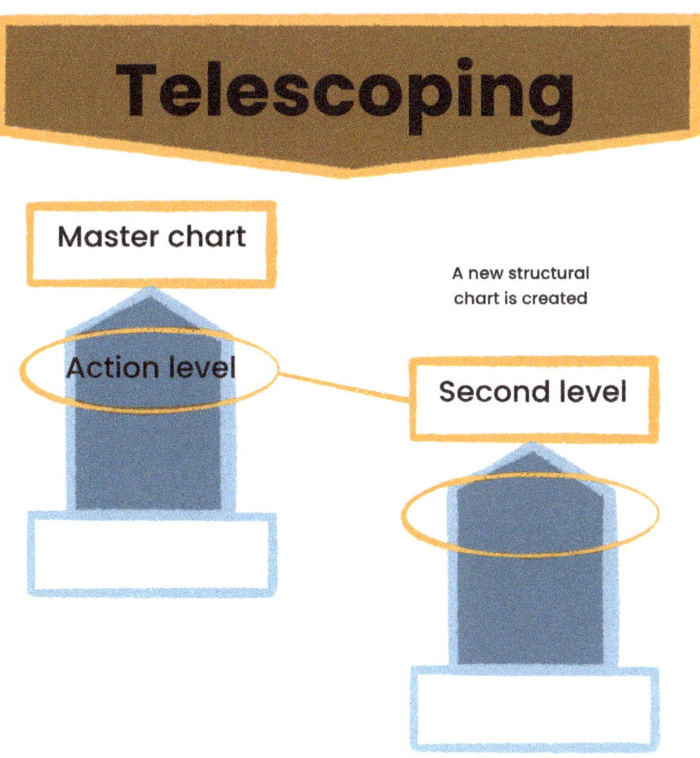

So, you have one master structural tension chart and further structural tension charts which are connected to the master one.

These structural tension charts are living documents and will need to be updated and negotiated as you move towards achieving your goal. The charts set the foundation for the work ahead to give you clarity to manage the work that needs to get done.

Let me tell you why you would be perfect for this

Throughout the year there will times when you need and want to pass on tasks and projects that land on your desk. This conversation is about how to do this in a clear and honest way.

Along with motivation, delegation is arguably one of the most misunderstood concepts I come across in my work. Every manager seems to want to know how to motivate people and reduce their workload.

Delegation is about passing on responsibility to someone to carry out specific tasks and projects. It is about passing on YOUR tasks and projects. Your direct report or anyone else in your team does not have to take on what you want to delegate. They usually will due to your position. You still need to sell it and be open to receiving a NO.

The following distinctions can be helpful when considering delegating your work. There are three actions you can take to pass on your responsibilities. It may or may not be delegation.

You can either Delegate, Distribute or Dump work.

Delegate – tasks or projects that YOU are responsible for doing. For example, attending your manager's team meeting. Presenting the 3-year strategic plan for your business unit. This is your work and no one is obliged to take it. You need to sell it.

Distribute – tasks or projects that is someone else's – usually your direct reports – responsibility to carry out. This is where you pass on the work directly. It can be as simple as forwarding an email. It could be a customer query that has landed in your voicemail. You distribute it to the person responsible for that customer or region in your team. If you get push-back from a team member. This gives you the opportunity to talk about the person's role and expectations you have for it.

Dump – tasks or projects you just want done by anyone with a heartbeat! Now, sometimes you just need to off-load some work because you have been called in by your boss to do something urgently. Or, it is a task like an annual event, such as the end-of-year party, which someone on the team needs to take. If no one takes it voluntarily, dump it on someone because you can!

Distribute and Dump conversations are usually straight forward. You distribute when a task clearly sits in another person's role. You dump when you really need to because you can.

On the other hand, delegating is a selling job. You are making a request and want a commitment. See the chapter "would be delighted if you can do this for me" in Conversations for Clarity.

When delegating, the following process can be helpful:

Before delegating, consider the following:

- What will I delegate? What outcome would delight me?
- Who shall I delegate to? What is in it for them?

While delegating, clarify the following:

- Task / Project
- Explain why you have chosen this person.
- What does success look like in terms of measures, quality, time?
- Agree what support you will offer.
- Questions and summarise – Ask the person to tell you what they have agreed to take on. A critical step.
- Agree next meeting.

Once the task is completed to your satisfaction

- Agree completion of task/project and offer feedback.

Remember, when delegating you are not leaving the person on their own. You need to be available to support and act as a sounding board during the execution phase. The chapters in Conversations to Deliver will be helpful for this.

Key messages from Conversations to Clarify

- A Conversation for Possibility acts like a bridge between a relationship in your network and committing to action with this person. A chance for two people to explore what is possible before making a decision to work together.
- There are two ways to commit to action with someone. Making a request or making an offer.
- Making a request is about asking someone for something that does not currently exist. Be clear on the goal that will delight you. Find someone who is competent and willing to take action to satisfy your request.
- Making an offer is about promising to deliver an outcome that will satisfy someone. You are promising to do everything in your power to achieve a satisfactory outcome.
- Knowing current reality in relation to our goal creates structural tension between where we are now and where we want to be. This tension seeks equilibrium which creates energy and momentum to reach our goal.
- Structural tension helps us define a plan on how we move from current reality to our goal. What we need to do. Who we want to help us and by when we need to have things done by.
- Delegation is when you ask someone to do some of your tasks.

Join Leadership Tuesdays to receive my weekly insights on leadership, navigating change and high-performing teams. Go to leadership4managers.com and sign up.

Conversations to Deliver

Purpose – To develop your people and get results that will delight you.

You are OK, what happened here is not OK

Feedback is data on performance. Information on how we are doing in relation to the goals we agreed on. Feedback is one type of conversation that a lot people talk about. It is rarely executed well or on a consistent basis. It is essential if you want a team member to achieve their goals that you have agreed with them. People want to know how they are doing. "Am I on track?" "Am I performing to expectations?" "Do I need to do anything differently?"

Setting goals at the beginning of the financial year, having a review after 6 months and then a final review at the end of the financial year is inadequate. Inadequate as a way of reviewing performance and getting the right work done if this is the ONLY thing you do.

Clear and regular feedback throughout the year makes 6-monthly and end-of-year reviews a lot easier. No surprises for anyone.

As we talked about in Conversations to Clarify, goals are commitments we undertake to create and deliver something that currently does not exist.

We need to be talking about the goals as well. Have your expectations changed regarding the goals you agreed on? How has current reality changed in relation to the goal? Does the person understand the goal and why he is being asked to carry it out? Feedback gets messy and ineffective if goals are not clear and/or constantly changing.

In preparation for giving feedback, you want to be clear on why you are giving it. Your intention should be to support the development and growth of the person. The person should feel that you want the best for them in the long term. This will make it more likely that the feedback will be accepted and reflected on instead of someone becoming defensive and rejecting what you say.

Not sure you even have to mention that you want to give some feedback. People generally think the worse when someone says "Can I give you some feedback?".

Can we get some time in to talk about your work, how you think you are doing and for me to share my thoughts on how I see you doing?

Take out the drama from the situation. You may have bi-weekly or monthly catch-ups. In which case, you can take it then.

Be clear on whether you want someone to stop doing something/do something differently OR whether you want someone to continue doing something.

Do not mix the two! Otherwise, your message may be mis-interpreted. Some people will focus on the negative and ignore the positive and some will focus on the positive and ignore the negative.

So, have a developmental intent and be clear on whether you want less of or more of something.

So, how to go about it. The following feedback model has been around a few decades and was originally created by the Center for Creative Leadership. I have adapted it to take into account the phases before and after giving feedback.

Preparation:

- Have a developmental intent, less of/more of something.
- Am I competent and credible in the domain I am offering feedback? Do I know what better looks like? If not, who is? Bring them into the conversation.
- Ground it: Based on what facts are you giving this feedback. "When you said/did…"
- Use Situation-Behaviour-Impact model.
- Be clear on why you are sharing the feedback.
- Be honest and kind.
- Include 'little' things.
- Give advice if requested.

During – SBI model:

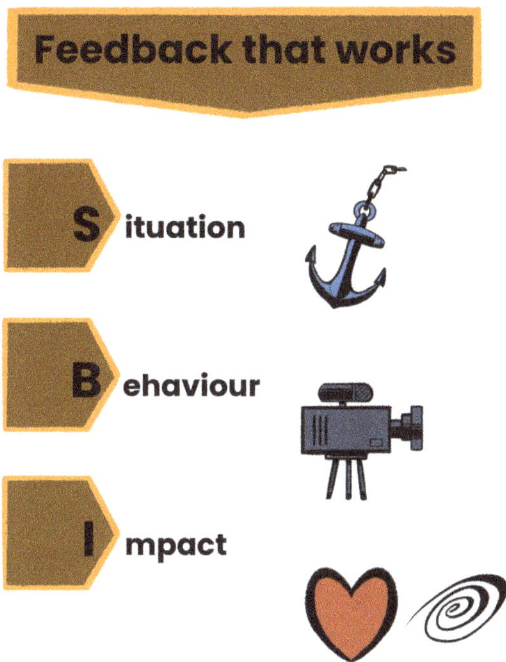

<u>Situation</u> – Where and when did it happen? Help orient the person so they take themselves to that place and time again.
"During yesterday's project Hercules meeting…"

<u>Behaviour</u> - What did the person do or say? It is like playing back a video recording of what happened.

"You arrived 12 minutes after the meeting had begun", "You have arrived between 5-15 minutes late on the previous 3 project Hercules meetings".

<u>Impact</u> – What impact has it had on you primarily? Then you can expand on the impact in areas such as the team, function, organisation, financial and reputation.

"I felt embarrassed and irritated. The project manager raised your late arrival with me and is wondering how committed you are to the success of the project".

At each stage, you don't want there to be discussion on whether something happened or not. "At this meeting, you did this and I felt". Nothing else. No one can argue with how you felt!

Be clear on the facts and open on the reasons.

Once you have shared the feedback, you want to listen to what the person makes of it. There may be good reasons why they have been late. Or maybe not. Hear the person out and listen to understand and show the person you understand what they are saying.

Understanding <u>does not equal</u> agreement.

You want to be clear on what happened and that it is not OK. The person may not like it and will likely take it personally. However, you both need to accept the SBI elements of the feedback. Then, and only then, can you move forward to discuss next steps and actions to improve the situation.

After:

<u>Action</u> – So, you have agreed on the feedback and the impact has been understood. Now what? If the person is competent in the area you are offering feedback, you can ask what she thinks will improve the situation. The person may know exactly what needs doing. If this is the case you may not need to make a suggestion. Otherwise, you will need to help out. After all, it is you that is not satisfied. Help the person satisfy your expectations.

You can make a request. We went through the elements of making a request in the chapter "I would be delighted if you can do this for me" in Conversations for Clarity.

You want her to stop doing or change the way she is doing something. What will make you satisfied or even delighted? Be reasonable. What do you want? How open are you to how it is done?

From this part of the conversation, you want a new commitment. "I will arrive on time to future project Hercules meetings". In other words, you want some offers.

You will want to have a follow-up conversation on this. In can be part of other 1-1 meetings you have.

As the giver of the feedback, you are responsible for letting the person know when the feedback is no longer relevant.

In the example above, this will happen when she starts turning up on time consistently to meetings. This demands clarity, what you are expecting and being competent to determine when feedback is no longer relevant.

If you are never satisfied then you will cause resentment in the person you gave feedback to and this is not good for a working relationship.

I like it, keep doing this

Feedback is generally associated with giving bad news to people. That dreaded moment when someone says 'Can I give you some feedback?'. The expectation is rarely that someone is going to say something complementary.

I notice the very same thing in my teaching of this subject. A large part of the focus is about how to give "constructive" or "negative" feedback to someone who is not performing as expected.

I would argue that we should be giving a lot more feedback that reinforces and recognises what is working well. It makes giving feedback on what is not working well a lot easier.

John Gottman PhD and Barbara Fredrickson PhD are two researchers worth noting.

John Gottman's decades-long study of what creates success in marriages points to the importance of the following:

- A 5-1 ratio of positive to negative interactions.
- Increasing positive interactions during conflict.
- Decreasing negative interactions such as blaming, defensiveness, contempt and stonewalling.

Now, I appreciate this concerns intimate relationships. However, I see these principles can be just as well applied to organizational relationships and teams.

If you have ever managed children's sports teams, you will be aware of the importance of reinforcing what is working well most of the time to encourage continued learning, creativity and experimentation. It works with adults too.

Now it needs to be genuine. You believe the person has potential and is capable of delivering to your expectations in her current role. Otherwise, you need to have another conversation about role-fit with them.

Feedback Ratio

Reinforcing: Stop doing/ Change

5:1

Reinforcing feedback can be in an email, text, direct message, at the coffee machine or in passing. You don't need to book a meeting for it. Include little things.

This will result in the person feeling more positive and engaged about their work and increase their confidence in role.

A ratio of 5-1 in reinforcing feedback. Feedback that focuses on what is working well may be challenging to start with. It is worth aspiring to. A good start would be for reinforcing feedback to be more than feedback about things you want someone to stop doing or change.

The result of this will be that people will be more open to feedback about things that are not working well as they will be feeling good about themselves and confident in their work and not feel under threat.

Thank You

You want more feedback in your organization, then get good at receiving it.

An element which is rarely focused on or talked about is how to receive feedback. This is important if you want to create a feedback culture where people feel safe to share what they think. You need to set a good example so that people feel comfortable to continue sharing feedback and receiving yours. If you respond in a defensive, dismissive or aggressive way the chances of getting more feedback are very low.

This is a conversation that may not be planned. You may find someone giving you feedback without warning or not following any particular feedback principles. There will something valuable to hear, so take the opportunity and find out what someone is thinking about you.

I have a list of tips to help you receive feedback in a way that will encourage people to keep giving you feedback.

Say thank you. It takes courage to give feedback. Show your appreciation. She did not have to give the feedback.

Listen – ask – listen. You have two ears and one mouth. Use them in that proportion. Sit back and take in what is being said and how it is being said. Ask questions, be curious and interested in the answer.

Clarification questions. If something is not clear, ask.

Receiving Feedback

Listen – Ask – Listen.

Do not accept or reject immediately.
Be curious and non-judgemental.
Ask clarification questions.
Be open and resist being defensive or blaming others.
Say "Thank You".

Be open and curious. There is always something of value to be learned from feedback.

Accept or Reject. You do not have to do either. Think of it like this. You are trying on a winter jacket in a store. You don't have to buy it. You can also buy it and try it on at home and then bring it back to the store.

Delivery may not be great. Remember not everyone is competent and confident giving feedback. Help the person clarify what they mean and be understood.

Close the loop. Once you have reflected on the feedback, go back to the giver and share your reflections on their feedback and thank them again for taking the effort of giving you feedback.

Before I tell you what I think

"Denis, you have two ears and one mouth, use them in proportion"

When you are talking about a piece of work with someone and your role is to help the person, you have two basic choices. Are you going to push your ideas and thinking or pull their ideas and thinking? In other words, are you going to use a directive approach or coaching approach? Which approach will you use most of the time?

With a coaching approach you are pulling or eliciting information and ideas from the person you are talking too. With a directive approach, you are pushing your ideas and information on to someone else.

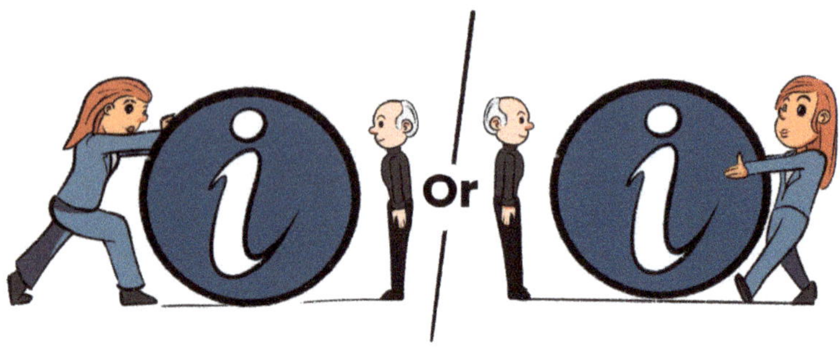

One of the more challenging conversations during delivery of a goal is the use of a coaching approach. The reason it is challenging is that you are doing less of the talking and less of the solution finding.

This can be difficult if you like the sound of your own voice or you have built a reputation and career as a problem solver/fixer.

When you are using a coaching approach most of the talking and solution finding is done by the other person. You want to help someone get really clear on the reality of their situation and their issue. Your job is to elicit or pull these ideas from the other person.

Through questioning, curiosity, presence and listening you are helping someone get clear on their reality and seeing an issue from a new perspective.

The skill of listening and asking curious questions is the main focus here.

So why would you want to use a coaching approach?

- People are more motivated to take action on solutions and ideas that they have come up with themselves.
- You find out the real cause of issues which results in better decisions and results.
- You get people to think for themselves and find their own solutions which can be better than your solution.
- Develop people by getting them to think for themselves, take manageable risks and learn.
- Increased engagement when people are consulted and listened to.

Let's be clear, a coaching approach is not to be used all the time. However, it can be a very good place to start most conversations.

If you are new to using a coaching approach as a leader, the following can be helpful when deciding if a coaching approach would work best.

When:

- The person is competent in the subject.
- You are not the expert.
- There is no one right answer.
- You want someone to think it through themselves.

- You can tolerate mistakes in the service of learning and development.
- It is a motivation or confidence issue.

When not to:

- Someone lacks technical knowledge and experience.
- There is a tried and tested way to solve an issue.
- The issue is about a breach of company values or ethics related.
- You are very stressed and pressed for time.

So, we have discussed what a coaching conversation is, why to use it and when/when not to use it. Let's move on to a model to help you structure a coaching conversation.

The GROW model. The GROW model is based on arguably the most popular coaching model I am aware of. Created by John Whitmore, in his classic book on coaching, "Coaching for High Performance". It was later refined to T-GROW by Miles Downey. It is not a linear model. You will end up jumping around.

You will notice similarities to what we discussed in Conversations for Clarity.

T-GROW model

Topic – What area (goal and/or subject) do want to focus on?
Goal – What do you want from the conversation?
Reality – Where are you now? What resources do you have?
Options – What options do you have?
Way Forward – What is your next step?

Topic - What area (goal and/or subject) do you want to focus on?

The purpose of this step to get focused on the subject area for the conversation. The subject area may be driven by you or your direct report. It can be helpful to connect the conversation to a goal which you have previously negotiated so you have something concrete to talk about.

Goal – What do you want from the conversation?

The problem presented is rarely the problem.

Getting clear on the goal of a conversation is critical. A clear goal – to start with at least – gives direction to the conversation. Something to hold on to and move towards. It can be an issue you want to talk about or something a colleague is interested in discussing. Be patient. Listen and be curious about what it is the person really wants to talk about. Don't assume the pre-meeting request to talk about project x is really just about project x. The person may really want to talk about a relational conflict in your management team. Hold the conversational goal lightly as it may change.

Reality – Where are you now? What resources do you have?

So, we now have the topic area, the goal for the conversation and now we want to explore the current situation. What has the person done so far? What is their understanding of the issue today? Help the person see the issue from as many perspectives as possible. Challenge their thinking, their interpretations and assumptions. By doing this you may find the goal of the conversation needs to change. Great, you now have a clearer goal that will be more helpful for the person.

If you give the Goal and Reality steps enough time, the next two steps will be more helpful and effective. Action will be based on a clear goal grounded in current reality. I have come to believe that these two steps done well are usually enough. People are usually smart enough to come up with options and an action if they are clear on what they want and where they are in relation to it.

Options – What options do you have?

In this phase of the conversation, you are turning your attention to possible ways to move forward. Help the person think as broadly as possible. Push them to think further.

Now, you will have some ideas as well. Save them till you have exhausted their ideas first. And then, share them lightly. For example, "From my experience, this was really helpful…" Most of the thinking and ideas should be coming from the other person. Combining ideas can be helpful too. Remember you are using a coaching approach because they are competent and you trust their judgement in the area you are talking about.

Way Forward – What is your next step?

So, what now? What action is the person prepared to commit to in view of what you agreed to talk about (Goal), a clearer understanding of the current reality (Reality) and after exploring different ways forward (Options). We are talking about a small step sometimes. Talking to somebody. Sometimes doing nothing. We are interested in the next step to move them towards their goal.

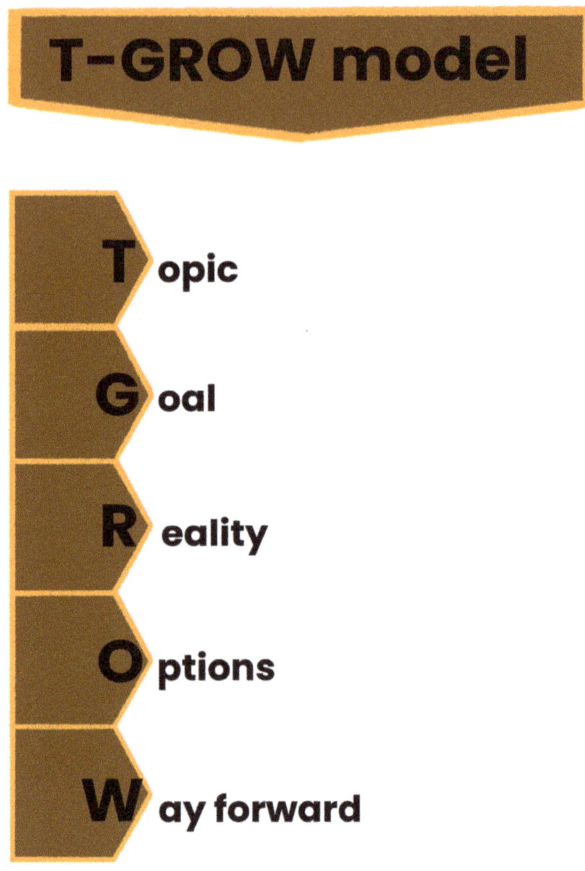

The following questions can help you during the different steps:

Goal questions

What do want to talk about?
What do want from this conversation?
What's the issue?
How can I help you?
What do you need?
How will you know this conversation has been helpful to you?

Reality questions

What is the situation right now?
What is getting in the way of what you want?
How clear are you?
Who is involved?
What resources – people/money – do you need?
Have you been in a similar situation before? What worked back then?
What have you done so far?
What is missing?

Option questions

What options do you have?
What could you do?
Anything else?

Who can help you?
What would be the next natural step?
What actions could you take?

Way Forward questions

What is your thinking on the subject now?
Are you ready to take action?
What are you going to do?
What can you commit to?
What support do you need?

What has helped me in the past

Now, you may find yourself in a situation where you need to offer advice and guidance.

Whenever you are doing most the talking you are probably using a directive approach.

As a manager and leader in your organisation, people look to you for advice and guidance with projects, tasks, career and personal issues. You may have an expertise which other functions need and you are seen as the go-to person.

Some guidelines when thinking about using a directive approach with someone.

When to be directive:

- The person is new in role and has some competence and knowledge in subject.
- You are the expert and there is agreed best practice in place.
- It would help to teach some principles and fill some knowledge gaps.
- You cannot tolerate mistakes in service of learning and development.
- An experience and knowledge gap needs filling.
- There is a critical deadline and you are very concerned that it will be missed.

When not to be directive:

- When the person is adequately competent and knowledgeable.
- There is no right solution.
- You are not the expert.
- You want someone to grow and develop and think for themselves.
- You want the person to be less dependent on you over time.

Most people I work with find being directive comes naturally. After all, people generally want to help. If asked it may seem rude not to share what you know.

The key question to be asking yourself is what approach is going to be most helpful in the long-term? Which approach should I use most of the time with this person on this particular subject? Now, if the subject changes, you may find you have to change your approach. For example, if someone is doing something for the first time and they want some guidelines, then being more directive would make sense. Then, if you moved to an area of their work where they are very experienced you will find a coaching approach more helpful.

It is bit like changing gears in a car. 1st gear is mainly directive and 6th gear is mainly coaching in its focus. Like the road conditions, you pay attention to where the conversation is going and change gears accordingly as smoothly as possible.

What someone may want and what they need are two very different things!

OK, we are done

All delivery of tasks and projects come to end. Sometimes we are delighted with the result. Sometimes just satisfied. And other times not satisfied at all.

The purpose of all the previous conversations is to increase the number of times you get delighted with the results of the work people do for you. And increase the number of times you delight people with the work you do.

So, did you get what you want? When a project or task is finished, you will want to have a conversation about it. Did the new product launch campaign combing digital and traditional media deliver the expected outcomes? Is the new purchasing agreement negotiated by procurement as you wanted it?

This is something that people involved in the goal have to agree on. The person who requested or offered something and the person who committed to executing the goal.

If both parties are satisfied then your satisfaction needs to be communicated to the person who executed the goal.

If you – the person who made the request – is not satisfied with the outcome, then you need to communicate this to the person responsible for executing the goal. Is there anything else that is missing that needs to be done before closing the task/project?

Assuming everything is OK after corrective action then the request is complete.

Now you have the opportunity to discuss what worked well, what could be improved next time and show appreciation for a completed request. Depending on how it went, use the feedback conversations for this purpose.

It is through successful completion of offers and requests that trust and credibility is built.

Key messages from Conversations to Deliver

- People want to know how they are doing. The good and the bad.
- Reinforce what is working well more often than telling people what is NOT working and needs to change.
- Telling people what is working well increases people's confidence and engagement in their work.
- When telling people what is not working, remember to let the person know when the feedback is not relevant anymore.
- There are two distinct ways of supporting someone with a goal; using a directive approach or a coaching approach.
- When a goal is complete let the person know how they did. What worked well and what could be better.

Join Leadership Tuesdays to receive my weekly insights on leadership, navigating change and high-performing teams. Go to leadership4managers.com and sign up.

In summary

In this Networked Age your success will depend on your ability to build mutually beneficial relationships over time. My intention with this book is to map out the conversations that will help build and maintain these relationships so that you are able to develop people and get results that delight you.

These conversations take practice. Getting good at anything takes practice.

Many of my clients have found these conversations helpful in building a valuable network as well as clarifying and executing meaningful goals for themselves and their organisations.

I hope these leadership conversations can do the same for you.

Warm wishes,

Denis
Gothenburg - May 20, 2021.

About the Author

Denis Goodchild is an international-renowned consultant supporting leaders confronting personal and business change. Since 2007, he has consulted in over 50 countries with multinational organisations. He has consulted in a wide range of sectors including: pharmaceutical, FMCG, food packaging and processing, charities, government agencies, utilities, travel, retail and car.

His consulting services include:

- The Leadership Mastermind which supports groups of leaders confronting personal and business change.

- A private coaching practice.

- Supporting leaders and their teams to become high performing by clarifying team purpose/goals, aligning ways of working, encouraging healthy conflict, and by better engaging key internal/external stakeholders.

He authors the popular Leadership Tuesdays messages where he shares insights and personal reflections on leadership, navigating change and high performing teams to a global community of leaders.

He lives in Gothenburg, Sweden with his wife and their 3 children.